West Hills STEM Academy
520 National Ave, Bremerton, WA 98312
(360) 473-4625

STEM Projects in MINECRAFT™

The Unofficial Guide to
Building Farms in
MINECRAFT™

JILL KEPPELER AND SAM KEPPELER

PowerKiDS press.

New York

Published in 2019 by The Rosen Publishing Group, Inc.
29 East 21st Street, New York, NY 10010

First Edition

Editor: Greg Roza
Book Design: Rachel Rising
Illustrator: Matías Lapegüe

Photo Credits: Cover, pp. 1, 3, 4, 6, 8, 10, 12, 14, 16, 18, 20, 22, 23, 24 (background) Evgeniy Dzyuba/
Shutterstock.com; p. 5 Irina Fischer/Shutterstock.com; pp. 6, 8, 10, 12, 14, 16 (insert) Levent Konuk/Shutterstock.com;
p.18 Marius G/Shutterstock.com; p. 22 Africa Studio/Shutterstock.com.

Cataloging-in-Publication Data

Names: Keppeler, Jill. | Keppeler, Sam.
Title: The unofficial guide to building farms in Minecraft / Jill Keppeler and Sam Keppeler.
Description: New York : PowerKids Press, 2019. | Series: STEM projects in Minecraft | Includes glossary and index.
Identifiers: LCCN ISBN 9781508169314 (pbk.) | ISBN 9781508169291 (library bound) | ISBN 9781508169321
(6 pack)
Subjects: LCSH: Minecraft (Game)–Juvenile literature. | Minecraft (Video game)–Handbooks, manuals, etc.–Juvenile literature.
Classification: LCC GV1469.M55 K47 2019 | DDC 794.8–dc23

Manufactured in the United States of America

CPSIA Compliance Information: Batch #CS18PK: For Further Information contact Rosen Publishing, New York, New York at 1-800-237-9932

Contents

Seeds of Learning

Minecraft is a sandbox game, which means players can explore the game world at their own pace, building things and altering the land. It's easier than exploring and building in real life. You don't have to worry about getting tired.

However, if you play in Survival **mode**, you do have to worry about getting hungry! An easy way to make sure you always have enough food is to build a farm. *Minecraft* farming is simpler than real-life farming, but you can still learn a lot about how to care for the land and make it produce good things to eat and use.

Building your own farm can be very useful. You can also build many other things. You could build a railroad to take your harvested crops to your *Minecraft* town!

Crops in Minecraft

You can grow a number of different plants in *Minecraft*, including wheat, carrots, potatoes, beetroots, melons, and pumpkins. Your in-game character can eat some of these products or you can use them to make other food items.

To grow wheat, beets, melons, or pumpkins, you need seeds. You can get wheat seeds by destroying *Minecraft* grass. You can find beetroot seeds in chests in different structures or growing in villages. You can get melon or pumpkin seeds by finding melons or pumpkins and using a crafting table. You can find most of these anywhere, but you can only find melons in a jungle **biome**.

MINECRAFT MANIA

When planted by the player, melons and pumpkins grow differently from other *Minecraft* crops. A stalk grows from their seeds and a melon or pumpkin grows from the stalk.

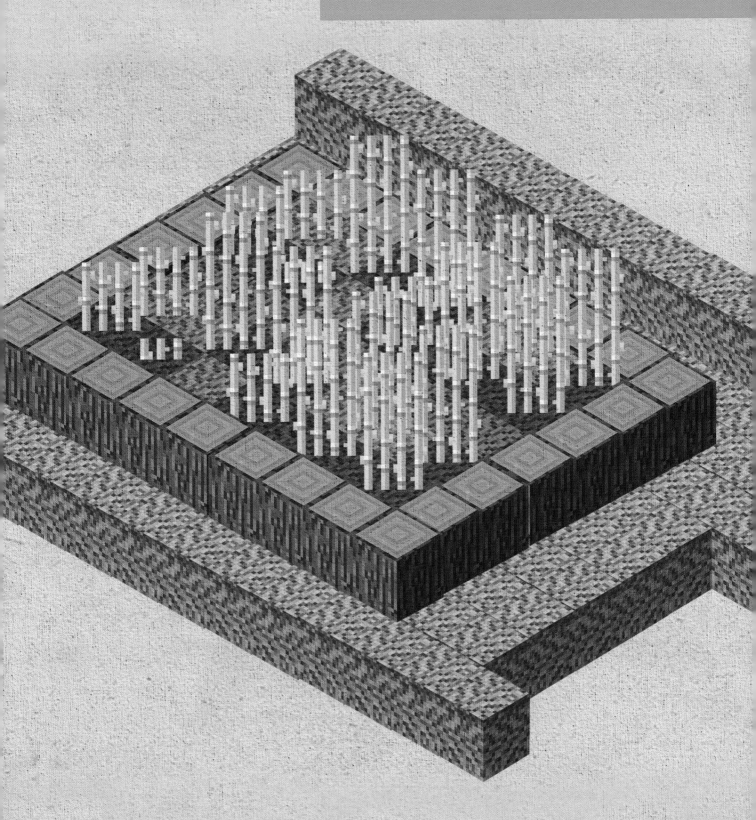

To grow carrots or potatoes, you plant one of the vegetables. You can find them growing in villages. Sometimes, zombies drop them when they're killed. The crop shown here is sugar cane.

Farming Principles

To grow crops, you first need a hoe. You can craft one with a stick and two wood **planks**, blocks of cobblestone, iron or gold **ingots**, or diamonds. You can use your hoe on a block of dirt or grass to turn it into tilled farmland.

It's most **efficient** to plant crops in farmland that has some form of **irrigation**. In *Minecraft,* this means that there's water at least four blocks away. A fully **hydrated** block of farmland is dark brown. It may take a little while for farmland to become hydrated, but seeds planted in it usually grow faster.

MINECRAFT MANIA

Crops also need a certain level of light to grow. This can be sunlight or the light from torches or glowstone. Without artificial light, your crops won't grow at night.

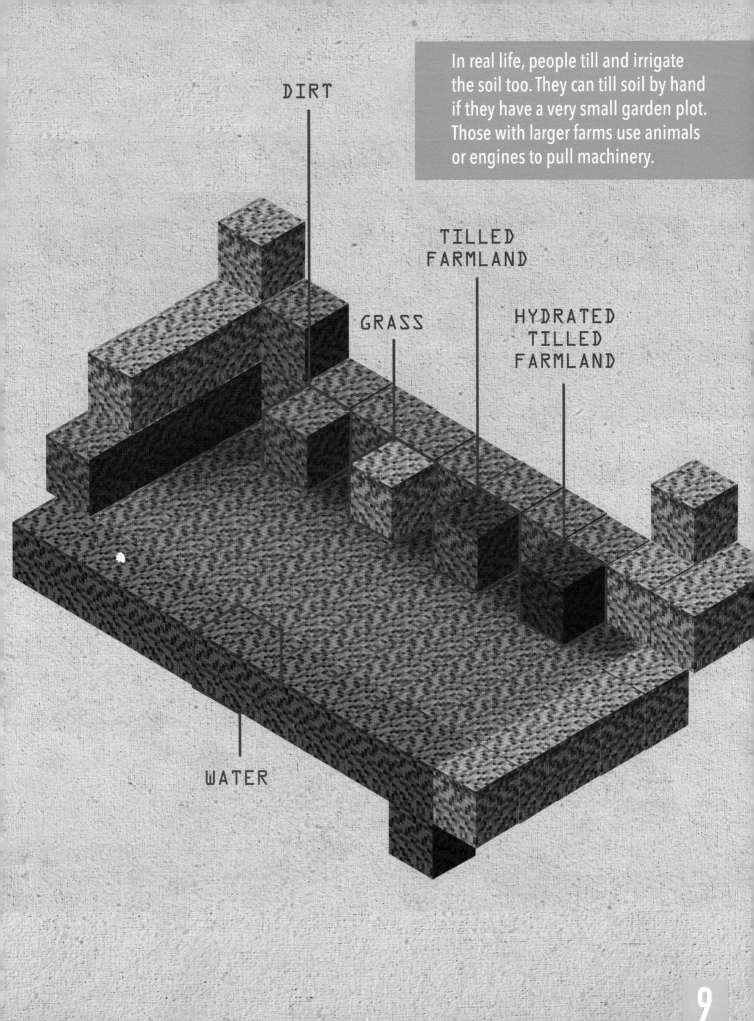

DIRT

TILLED
FARMLAND

GRASS

HYDRATED
TILLED
FARMLAND

WATER

Efficient Plans

If you don't have a bucket in which to carry water, you can plant crops right at the edge of a body of water in *Minecraft*. Once you have a bucket, however, you can create your own farm plot near your home.

Because one block of water will hydrate farmland up to four blocks away, your farm can be nine blocks by nine blocks with only that one water block in the middle. However, you may wish to create pathways on which you can walk among your crops. Think about what kind of farm you want. Use math to create an efficient **design**!

MINECRAFT MANIA

Crops won't grow if a player isn't within a certain range of blocks. This varies depending on your *Minecraft* settings. If you really need a certain type of crop to grow, stay close!

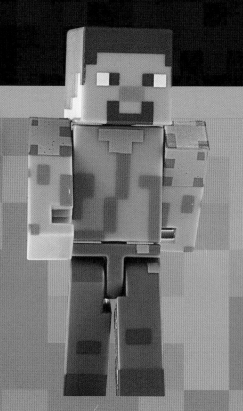

If you jump or fall on crops, the farmland will return to being dirt and the dirt will drop the crops. Be careful!

11

Harvest Time

It's hard to **predict** how long it will take crops to grow. Wheat, potatoes, carrots, and beetroots each have eight stages of growth. Each stage can take 5 to 35 minutes. Wheat's finished growing when it's a darker green-brown. The vegetables are done when you can see their tops above the ground.

If you need to speed up your crop growth, you can use bone meal made from bones on your crops. When harvested, a wheat plant drops zero to three seeds and one piece of wheat. Carrot and potato plants drop one to four vegetables each. Melons, however, drop slices.

MINECRAFT MANIA

You can't directly eat *Minecraft* wheat, but you can use it to make bread or as an ingredient in cookies or cake. Similarly, a pumpkin is an ingredient in pumpkin pie.

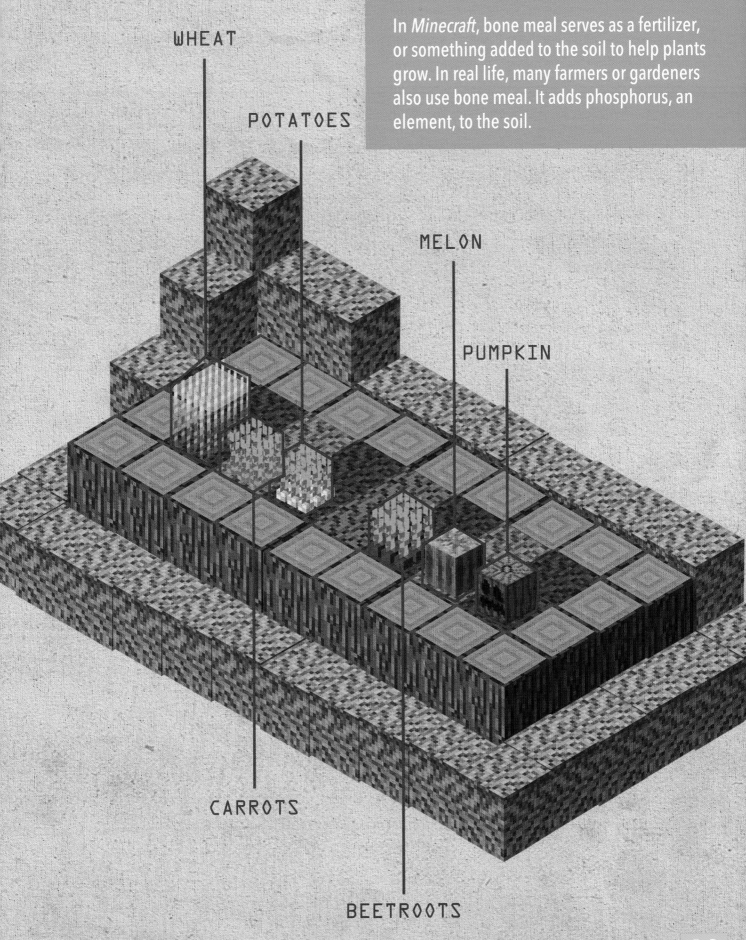

WHEAT

POTATOES

MELON

PUMPKIN

In *Minecraft*, bone meal serves as a fertilizer, or something added to the soil to help plants grow. In real life, many farmers or gardeners also use bone meal. It adds phosphorus, an element, to the soil.

CARROTS

BEETROOTS

Going High Tech

Farming is pretty simple in *Minecraft*, but you can make it more high tech if you want! You can have a small garden plot or a huge farm with separate plots for each crop. Some people use mine carts and tracks to help them **transport** harvested crops throughout their farm or to their home or a storage site.

If you know how to use redstone in *Minecraft*, you can build machines that will **automatically** harvest (and sometimes transport) your crops for you. Many of these designs use water to flood the ground and send the plants to a hopper, or a device that collects them.

MINECRAFT MANIA

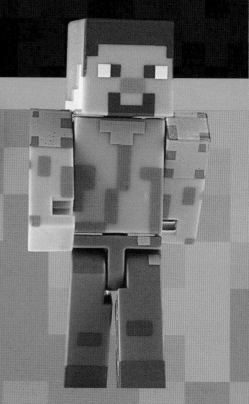

You can also grow sugarcane, trees, and mushrooms in *Minecraft*. These plants work a little differently than other crops, however. For one thing, you don't need tilled farmland for them.

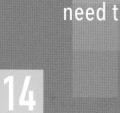

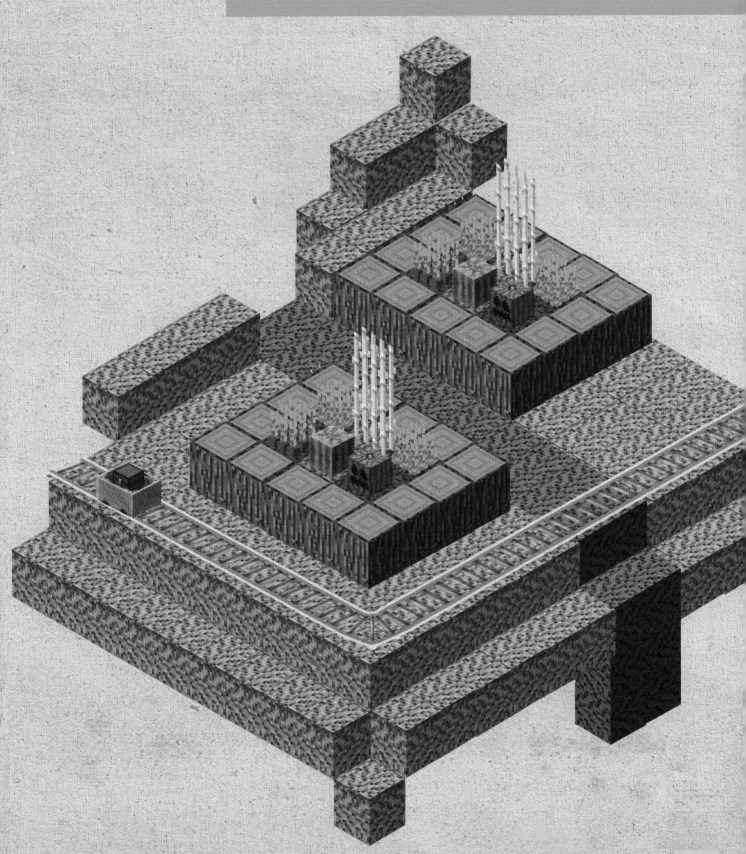

Livestock in Minecraft

You can also keep livestock on your farm in *Minecraft*. The game has cows, pigs, chickens, and sheep. You can get meat from each of these animals, as well as **resources** such as leather, milk, feathers, eggs, and wool. Use seeds to draw chickens to your farm. Use wheat to draw cows or sheep. Pigs will follow players holding carrots, potatoes, or beetroots.

At first, you can build a fenced-in pen with a gate to hold your livestock. Add a small fenced-in area with its own gate just outside the main pen. That way, if anything escapes, it won't go far.

MINECRAFT MANIA

Minecraft also has donkeys, mules, horses, and llamas, which can be tamed and are useful as transportation. To tame a horse, ride it (with nothing in your hands) until it doesn't buck you off.

A simple wooden fence will keep your livestock from wandering. As you get more resources, you could also build a big barn.

Growing Your Stock

Once you have at least two of a livestock animal, you can breed them, or cause them to make a baby animal. It takes baby animals about 20 minutes to grow up, and you can't get meat or other resources by killing baby animals.

To breed cows, feed each adult cow a piece of wheat, making sure they're standing near each other. You'll see hearts, and then a baby cow will appear. You can also use wheat for breeding sheep. Use seeds for chickens and potatoes, carrots, or beetroots for pigs. After about five minutes, you can breed them again.

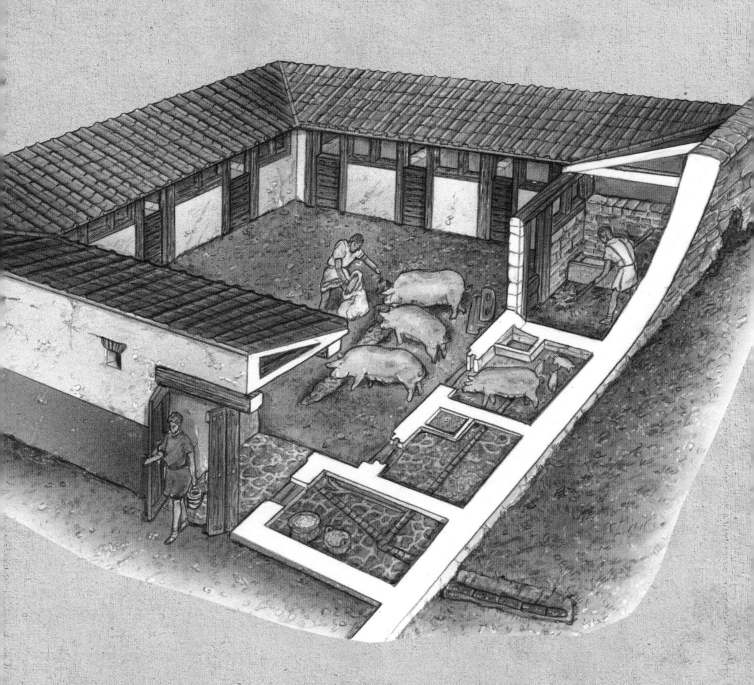

To make sure you have a steady supply of animals, always have two adults of each kind.

A Plentiful Harvest

Agriculture, or the science and practice of raising crops and livestock, has made a huge difference in human history. It made civilizations possible as people settled down in one place instead of constantly traveling to follow and hunt wild animals.

In *Minecraft*, farming makes it possible for you to settle down in one place, too. It means you don't have to worry about hunting for food all the time. If you have a well-designed farm, you'll always have a source of food. That means you can pay more attention to exploring your world and building creative new *Minecraft* structures!

If you can build a farm like this in *Minecraft*, you'll never go hungry again! Then you can save your time for things like exploring.

Making Mods

You can make your *Minecraft* creations even more exciting with modifications, or mods. Using a computer program called ScriptCraft, you can create new blocks, change the way the game functions, and make your own games. Imagine what you could build! Would you like to grow different fruits and vegetables, such as bananas or corn, in *Minecraft*? You could even create new animals, such as reindeer or goats.

If you're interested in learning how to create mods in *Minecraft*, visit the website below. You'll find the information needed to get started with ScriptCraft and build your own *Minecraft* mods.

https://scriptcraftjs.org

Glossary

automatically: Happening on its own, without being directly controlled.

biome: A natural community of plants and animals, such as a forest or desert.

design: The pattern or shape of something. Also, to create the pattern or shape of something.

efficient: Capable of producing desired results without wasting results, time, or energy.

hydrate: To add water to something.

ingot: Metal made into a shape for storage or transportation.

irrigation: The supplying of water to land by man-made means.

mode: A form of something that is different from other forms of the same thing.

plank: A heavy, thick board of wood.

predict: To guess what will happen in the future based on facts or knowledge.

resource: Something that can be used.

transport: To convey from one person or place to another.

Index

Websites

Due to the changing nature of Internet links, PowerKids Press has developed an online list of websites related to the subject of this book. This site is updated regularly. Please use this link to access the list:
www.powerkidlink.com/stemmc/farms